Head and Heart

Don Garrett

Published by New Generation Publishing in 2019

Copyright © Don Garrett 2019

First Edition

The author asserts the moral right under the Copyright, Designs and Patents Act 1988 to be identified as the author of this work.

All Rights reserved. No part of this publication may be reproduced, stored in a retrieval system or transmitted, in any form or by any means without the prior consent of the author, nor be otherwise circulated in any form of binding or cover other than that which it is published and without a similar condition being imposed on the subsequent purchaser.

ISBN: 978-1-78955-601-8

www.newgeneration-publishing.com

New Generation Publishing

Contents

A Friendship 1
Through Emotions 2
Under the Stars 3
Inner Voice 4
Flickering Candles 5
Silhouette 6
Lifetime in a moment 7
A Stirring within me 8
Seeking Home 9
Flawless Beauty 10
Spectre of Love 11
Midsummer Dream 12
Inside 13
Three Hearts Rent 14
Thou art Beautiful 15
The Birth of Love 16
Shamed and Humble 17
Missing 18
Walk beside me 20
Our own silent world 21
Decisions 22
Flower for Giving 23
Ice meets Fire 24
From Nowhere 25
Feelings 26
Warm Comfort 27

Praise for a Heartbeat	28
What do you see in me?	29
English Rose	30
The Symphony	31
The Challenge	32
You Came Alive	33
Foolish Thoughts	34
Harmony	35
When sweet darling buds?	36
Longing	37
A Request	38
Empty Awareness	39
Mirrored Heart	40
Of You	41
Through the eyes	42
If	43
Whispers	44
Image of Aphrodite	45
Imagining You	46
Sadly	47
Missing the Music	48
Plain Walls	49
In You	50
Elastic Minds	51
Two Trysts	52
Forever Entwined	53
Misty Mornings	54
Empty Memories	55
Turned Emotions	56
Effecting a mind	57

Offering	59
Flawed Hope	60
When words fail	61
Should I?	62
Dreadful Fear	63
Fearful Companion	64
From Whence we came	65
An ill wind blows	66
A Last Goodbye	67
The Final Kiss	68

A Friendship

I sense your presence although youre not there
Knowing always that you will be near to care
Perhaps well not see each other for many a day
But trust is our strength that we share in this way.

When first we met those many years ago
Strangers we were- soon a friendship did grow
Yet life has its way- our lives took different trails
Soon months turned to years and somehow our friendship prevailed.

We meet on occasions sometimes on the street
Warm smile firm handshakes make plans and a time where we again can meet
Then just like yesterday our conversation steadily flows
Exchanging life stories - families and children how quickly they grow.

Its just like the old days as we look back in time
Remembering our follies and we laugh at those climes
Capturing fleeting memories, of people we have met
Enjoying our moments in our tales a d times we have spent.

Our understanding of friendship is not written down
Just simple people who fate let us meet and a bond was bound
For wherever our travels in this wonderful world of ours
We remember each other fondly for we have a friendship beyond earthly towers.

Through Emotions

Do you understand pain?
Not from cuts or bruises,
From inside it became
Emotional arousing or deep melancholy.

Do you feel empty?
When lovers pass you by
Look for the rainbow
When rain leaves a blue sky?

Do you understand love?
Whereupon the body tingles
Does your blood race
And your temperature rises ?

Do you sob and sigh
As a memory goes by
Rue and regret
Yet never forget?

Do you untie the cord?
When you have lost mutual accord?
Stand deep in the shadows
And become pale and sallow?

Under the Stars

How sad to feel the past glide by the face
When sunlit clouds hover on cobalt skies,
How eerie to hear the gulls haunting call
And watch in silence as years past falls.

Once graceful to glide across the floor
Now humbled shuffling to the doors.
As in haste we welcome tomorrow with open arms
To re-live in memory, life's golden chance.

Those eyes that once sparkled so
Now wears glasses to bring out the inner glow.
Soft slender hands that once with pleasure thrilled
Struggles hard to hold a beaker to stop the spills.

The shimmering moon against black velvet night
The twinkling stars dancing with delight
And loved ones sigh, and try to claim the sweetest flight.
Before dawn's gossamer tendrils veils the beautiful sight.

Inner Voice

Like the echo in the night
As the wind howls through a crack
And thunder hurts the ears
Bright white lightning sears the eyes
And rain stings the naked skin.
Sensitivity seems a silly thing,
Yet harken to the inner voice
The one which always seeks the truth
Wise choice it seems
Yet the head screams it has no choice
So naked stands against the wall
Shadows thrown to make one tall
Though shrinking violet one has become
Scared of what the future offers some,
Outside nature clamours for the debt to be paid
This time only your minds thoughts
Are there for you to save.

Flickering Candles

Eyes meet across the chasm of space,
Pupils dilate while the heart beats at a faster pace.
The body warms, while the mouth goes dry.
Should the moment pass you would then wonder why.

How crowded the room appears to be
Yet cocooned in silence, set apart and free.
Like flickering candles with the flame so bright
In the tender, mercurial phase that is a delight.

Fanned by passion, forged by a need,
Two people stand alone, in the universe of greed
Seeking peace and togetherness with hope supreme,
For the flame of pleasure to burn eternal, forever clean.

As tempestuous seas, love rages and roars
Sometimes battered, the pain leaves only sores,
Then as the sun rises to becalm the seas
Tenderness awakes, rekindles passion to please.

Carefree and unbridled hands do clasp
Breath is taken, expelled with a gasp.
All this in a moment of the first glance
A lifetimes journey, will the dream last?

Silhouette

Ah! Bliss, you stand before me
I soak up your beauty
Warm, how it feels
Do opposites' attract?
Chances are slim, like your shape,
Be yourself- best way to be
Should you like me, ah! Ecstasy.
Always in my thoughts since we met
The effect seems to be so profound
From my side only- Ah! Forget it
Too good for me, sure but…….!
Foolish really maybe I'm not your kind?
Warm are my feelings and I can't forget
How sad it is when you left
I just have the memory, of your silhouette.

Lifetime in a moment

No, I will never forget you although briefly we just met,
To soon we parted with many a regret.
How happiness came upon me with just a tender smile,
And a lifetimes loving arrived in such a little while.

Amidst the throng we stood alone
Shared the pleasurable moments on our own.
Eternity is too short a time with you to share
To explain in depth of how much for you I care.

Oh dearest heart the one for me which is forbidden.
Where images captured of when one was smitten,
To hold in memory where the joy is exciting
And the fragrance of life's love is so enticing.

No time to hold those small and delicate hands,
No time to tenderly kiss those inviting lips,
Just time to drown in mesmerising eyes so deep
Inside liquid pools, my secret, long must I keep.

A dream to hold you in my arms so tight,
To hear you laugh out loud in delight.
To catch ones breath as spirits soar,
Relive those precious moments again once more.

For I must turn the other cheek
Leave discreetly, silently, and do not speak.
Of how my pain does sear my soul
For love in life, one does not control.

A Stirring within me

I don't think I will fall for you in the conventional way,
My words ramble in the oddest order
So I close my eyes and to the heavens I pray.
It is the little things that endear me to you,
How on the phone you uh-huh so softly
That sets a stirring within me so I get a tickly cough.
I miss the way you press into me
Your warmth a comfort and haven you see.
Your coyness, I know, is the trap to ensnare
To be honest, with you, I am happy to share.
I feel great when you hold my hand
Although sometimes, you, I don't understand,
Your kisses are swift that leaves me wanting more.
How enjoyment I get when your body I explore.
I love it when we walk close side by side,
I find in you I can confide
I don't need to think of you each moment of the day
For your always with me and I like it that way.
Convention I feel is not for us-but being quite normal
Sometimes we both do have a curse and a cuss.
What I see in you I cannot honestly say,
A warm, comfortable feeling makes me want to stay.
Perhaps we will learn how to harness our thoughts
Understand each other's needs so wars are not fought.
When I read this I have a feeling in my chest,
In the heart region I must confess.
I'm glad you have walked into my life
A little bit of sunshine, bound to be a bit of strife.
You know I cannot hold onto a verse
I sadly fear there is something much worse,
I have felt much happiness since you came along
Yet this feeling within me, I'd lose you were I not strong.
I miss you with pain, so I'll politely ask
Is there another glass of wine in your cask?

Seeking Home

Where do my thoughts go when I'm all alone?
They follow your perfume- follow you home.
Comfort and joy waits beside you there
It is my dream, I want you to share.

To bask in your smile,
Sit with you awhile,
Listen to your musical voice
And inside, my heart will rejoice.

But, a spirit I can never be
So here I stand in solitary,
Blown by the wind no direction is known
Seeking a place that I could call home.

Flawless Beauty

Look at me my lovely
Let me see your soul
Show eternal fidelity
And love you can't control.

I see your heart beating
An echo of my own
If fate has pointed out a reason
Why we two should not be a whole.

You are the image of my dream
Incarnate, my wonderful queen
Should I kneel before thee?
You touch my heart and set it free.

My loveliest of lovelies
In my heart I want you to be
Safe and warm forever
Until the end of eternity.

Drape your arm around my shoulder
Press close against my chest
Feel my love stirring
Let nature do the rest.

My eyes see you as a flawless beauty
The way nature meant you to be
Soft eyes, warm smile sweet lips
Take me to the tip of ecstasy.

Spectre of Love

And as the loves dream slowly walks away
Hopes are dashed and words no longer make her stay.
Where emptiness clings like the morning mist
Soon to be dispersed when sunlight plants her warming kiss.

With heavy heart no longer beating
Eyes that dim as the light is now fleeting,
Once strong pulse of life that kept life's blood stirring
Now blanched white as colours become blurring.

What held love strong in dreams alone
Leaving empty shells that could be cloned.
As time and energy were truly spent
Where words were spoken and truly meant

No glimpses now, for the ghostly spectre disappears
Leaving shard like splinters piercing tears
While the soul cries out for a lover who,
Will be the anvil to forge romance so true.

Midsummer Dream

Oh! Warm and tender could you be?
When a feeling seems perfect just for me,
As eyes that hold a deep desire
Where mortals hope to aspire,
Each thought could be the magic key
Unlock a heart confined to obscurity.
If sadness in this world should be
Then free me to enjoy with you, tranquilty.
I see a face, warm and tender too
A heart that beats for one so true.
Each step along the path to tread
Joy and happiness not fear and dread.
When hands do clasp and warmth floods through
Each thought is yours, each thought is true.
A chance to smile, a chance to love
Embrace the pleasure and fly like the dove.
When blood flows freely as a spirit stream
Enjoy each night in the midsummer dream.

Inside

As the sun breaks through the winter chill
How crisp the air brings shivers that thrill
All snugly wrapped with icicles on eyelashes
Footfalls crunch on snow, no puddles for splashes.

With cheeks a rosy red from air sharp as pins,
Nose with sniffles as needles seem to prick the skin
The smile shines through to break the winter spell
To the chosen one beguiled, to the one who fell.

A tender smile to melt ones heart
Shining eyes that twinkle like the stars,
And the face that welcomes and beckons you home
No reason now to wander, no needs to roam.

The single look that spoke a thousand words
When a kiss sent the message to my awakened nerves
I am here to stay the message clearly said
Inside one came alive, hope eternal instead of dread.

Cheek to cheek that which was so very brief
Dispelled the anguish, dispelled all grief.
The tender moment of your warm embrace
Broken too swiftly, left nonplussed, red faced.

Oh! Woman of beauty, of cheerful grace
Look at me lovingly and tell to my face,
The words that my ears long to hear
Give me good tidings make my heart full of cheer.

Three Hearts Rent

If my eyes could look into a soul
What would they see?
Happiness or sorrow
Sunshine or dark as could be?
Take away the pulse of life
Would we be addled with strife?
No longer a heartbeat
Just existing in a world of make believe.
Death is so final
Where understanding and acceptance
Keeps one company.
Yet a forced parting endows a lifetimes
Sentence of living death!
Where are ones children from a union of love?
Abiding with their mother
As the judgement has been done.
What of the father whose love is also pure?
Ostracised, on the other side of the door.
Stolen lifetime of his children
What wrong did he do?
Suffered the woman's infidelity,
But kept his dignity.
The price is too dear that is his fear,
Living in isolation now unable to share
Not wanting a lover too scared to care.
Where are the memories?
Of their life chapters, not seen by my eyes
Unable to be there should they want to cry.
Who are the victims of her greed and contempt?
Three lives ruined, three hearts rent.
Oh how heartless cold and contrite
How does one slumber through each night?
This burden placed on shoulders so small
Does this the final judgement make you stand tall?

Thou art Beautiful

Then kiss me my sweet
Let our souls together meet,
Eyes seek truth and hope
Heart's throb in eternal hope.

The temple of adornment stands
As angels descend and softly lands,
A warm embrace sets hearts beating
A fire's aglow, the body heating.

A tingle, a shiver, shortness of breath
At hearing the heartbeats inside the chest.
For thou art beautiful in my eyes alone
I stand before you to welcome you home.

The Birth of Love

It was when I held you close to me,
Scarce moments from when you were born.
Snuggled in a blanket, just to keep you warm
So close we were a child and a dad.

Each day we grew together
The ties that bond grew ever stronger,
Love from dad was evident
The child somehow knew.

And slowly as the mind developed
The child learnt something new.
Always seeking comfort in arms
That gave love and protected too.

Years passed.- the bond between the two
Remained steadfast, strong and true.
Until one day a shadow hovered over them.
Cold and damp, the sun no longer shone
And soon all the love was gone.

The memory does linger
The hope will always burn,
While the love remains eternal.
But the light of life dims and flickers

Shamed and Humble

I saw the shadow pass through your eyes
The pain I caused you could not disguise
How shamed and humble I became
Yet you walked tall as I held the blame.

The pride I felt at your demeanour
My love grew strong became the fervour
Now cast aside as a broken toy
Looking on no longer is a joy.

Tis pain and sorrow my just reward
Must I die by my own sword?
For carrying a torch my flame burnt bright
All I sought was for your delight.

Now I suffer at my own hand
Retributions lost and I understand
As I cut you to the very quick
The trust, once firm has lost its grip.

How deep your pain I cannot fathom
To heal your wounds then I should have them.
To carry the scars to admit my guilt
Try to refill the cup of love I spilt.

Missing

It is the essential part
That makes life the reason,
Why it is a joy
to wake up and smile,
brings the warmth
to the eyes.
The tenderness to the lips
gentleness of the touch
safely in the biggest hug
hidden from all view.
Pain in the heart
in knowing what is
missing.
A hello and warm kiss
from those who gave
all the immeasurable bliss,
sometimes the anguish,
sometimes the pain
brought you the sunshine,
clouds and the rain.
Made memories all the same.
And always, always complained.
Sweet innocence cannot be bottled
nor sold for any price,
yet loneliness eats at a soul
as the eyes grow dim
and weary while
memories begin to fade,
recognition becomes a blur,
soon words begin to slur
as age takes over.
Lost time is the empty carousel
for round and around
the mind rambles, seeking

light within the shade,
chasing ghosts from time long past
hiding the truth that in
dying - love forever will last.

Walk beside me

Will you walk beside me in the spring time?
Through the valley where the air is sweet
Amongst the yellow coloured flowers,
That bends before your feet?
While the sun gives warmth to the meadows carpet of green.

Shall the trees hear your lilting, melodious laughter?
Or could the leaves dance along to the tune?
Would the birds join in with a chorus of their very own?
As the gentle breeze hums softly as it flows.

Perhaps the sparkle in your eyes could diminish the golden sun?
Surely your lovely exuberance will entrance everyone
The pleasure of your company, the closeness of us two
Life is now so pleasurable, because I am with you.

Our own silent world

Its early days between you and I
Yet my head and mind are full of you
I know of how you are in a deep conversation
I seem to have you now as my main consideration.
You, you, always you, which to me is unclear
We speak on a cell phone -always in an ear.
I want to see those eyes of yours
Of how they will react
When I say something naughty
Or make a silly wisecrack.
Already I love the softness of your voice
And the sounds of your musical laugh - yet
I'd like to see the sparkle in your eyes
See a broad smile on your face
Feel the warmth of your closeness
And never rush the pace.
I'd like to walk along a path with you holding my hand
People would surely look, perhaps they'll understand
How they felt when feelings overtook themselves
And forgot the whole of the world
Yes, there would be just the two of us
Inside our own silent world..

Decisions

Least eyes shed tears of sadness
And the heart fails to beat.
As air exhaled admits defeat
A soul will die through madness

Decisions made under duress
An empty shell- now loose- aimless
Not purified or sanctioned
Sullied- broken now malfunctioned

Ghosts or spectres-swirling mist
Timeless - motion cannot resist
Ravaged by cruel cold winds
Dreams-hopes do not exist.

Flower for Giving

You have blossomed well my love
As a flower with petals gleaming
Eyes so clear and bright
A smile that is beaming.

Crowning glory is your hair.
Dark, lustrous shimmering- alive.
Infectious to life-confidence brimming
Hopes alive romance for giving.

When fully bloomed
What a flower you'll be
Delicate, shapely,
Developed quite beautifully.

And with your pollen
As sweet nectar be
Should your flower be for giving?
Then my love- Share it with me.

Ice meets Fire

I shall strive to remain ice-cool
Not to be taken as anybodies fool,
For when she breezed by with eyes aglow
No shame or humility did she show.

Hair short and spiky, white and bright as snow
Blue eyes that shone, with an inner flow
Of assuredness that emanated like a flame
A goal to achieve. Understand no blame or shame.

A smile that brightens up the day,
Teeth so white they sparkle anyway,
With skin as pure as driven snow
Men's hearts melt swiftly, does she know?

The figure slim, with curves so true
Made to capture eyes as she passes through,
Perfume sweet and with a laugh that makes a heart sing,
While down the spine, shivers tingle with added zing.

A fire burns deep down within a soul,
While ice melts swiftly beyond control.
And like the night as dawn appears
She is gone, perhaps forever, one truly fears.

From Nowhere

Odd that we should meet this way
For there is a familiar resemblance
That strikes a cord and wants to force its way
From deep within the recesses of the mind.
As one stumbles from memories that's so tired and aged
Where fond themes are stored from times when young and bold.
Each story held as precious jewels,
The pearls of wisdom sometimes unfold.
To hear the laughter strong and full of love,
Where tears fell down because of glee
Whilst sat around the Christmas tree.
Each candle perched upon a birthday cake
Brings back sad memories, makes the soul truly ache.
No longer young, grown in health and looks
No more stories read from nursery books,
The eyes that looked upon life with hope
Seem dull and lifeless, from the lack of love.
Perhaps searching for the protecting hand
With fingers entwined so true and strong
This factor grew to become the bond.
Then from nowhere, by chance we met
The smiles of love shared between us, was not of regret.
Perhaps, if time would us allow
To forge again the bond we knew so well,
Where guidance between us would slowly grow
The faith and hope upon us each would bestow,
Then life again would be bright and full of hope.

Feelings

I bend when strong winds blow
I quiver through the hurricane
I get soaked through a thunderstorm
I bake when the sun gets strong
I freeze when snows are deep
And through all this, I think of you.
My feelings grow each passing season
I have searched the lowlands and highlands
Lonely and cold, my warmth is you
I seek your hand, your heart, your love
I long to hold you close, feel your warmth
Smell your fragrance, feel your skin
Learn the signs from within your eyes
Be comforted by your closeness
Become strong within your embrace
Feel beloved and wanted by only you
For I offer a love that is unsurpassed
Yet unrequited as it seems for you know not I
Worlds apart, oceans divide mountains a barrier
Millions surround you, yet I see only you
Your aura shines a golden hue
My love, my love I seek only you.

Warm Comfort

Silently and unseen, untouched and unexpectedly,
The net is cast the trap is set, now patience is required.
Who is the hunter, who is the prey? Now the heart has been desired.
The realisation of a wondrous feeling one can expect.

It captures the imagination it fires up the soul
Everything is achievable to realise this wonderful goal,
Sight, oh! The vision so warm, tender and yet,
Lost for a few fleeting moments, no time to suggest or request.

A moment of dalliance, a brief interlude,
The warm smile of recognition leads me to conclude,
A friendship is growing perhaps it will lead to more.
Yet, the sadness grows heavy when alone again once more.

The thoughts in the head leaves a stirring deep in the soul
Each nerve end tingles and all the senses are alert,
As the pulse starts racing perspiration soaks ones shirt.
Tongue gets tied and words fail, now, who will help to console?

Your image, frozen in my mind, pictures I find so divine,
From the toss of your hair to the brief glance from your eyes,
How the stomach does tighten and a leap as the heart sighs.
How I find warm comfort in watching you is sublime.

I long for the look that says I am yours,
Wait for the handclasp that is so warm, firm and sure.
Long for the tenderness of our first loving kiss
And the warm embrace where I shall find perfect bliss.

Praise for a Heartbeat

Then praise be for a heartbeat
Led by the eyes, emotions can begin.
The image then engrained upon the brain
In a honeycomb cell is contained.

A chamber set for love to reside
One that stands alone with pride.
A cell for speech where foolish words spill forth
And another for the tongue- tied of course.

The tunnel to contain the fire within the belly,
One for steady nerves that somehow turn to jelly.
A tap, to regulate the sweat glands on and off,
Another so similar to soothe the tickly cough.

Emotions are a fickle thing, that seems to start in spring,
A friendly smile gives the body an extra zing.
Is the heart attuned to nature's way?
Or do Homo sapiens have their own say?

What do you see in me?

Oh! Lovely lady with skin soft and warm
How come you turn to me?
With my greying hair, not as it used to be
What do you see in this old man worn?

Time has passed but I rode it true
I lost in love-that time I do rue
Alone, I withdrew from society
Kept myself in true sobriety.

Years did pass-I stayed alone
Not entreating love- but my eyes did roam
Passion slept through each season
Soon I forgot- for no other reason.

I gazed upon many pretty women
Dormant did my heart abide
Until the time on you-my eyes spied
A fluttering thrill sent my heart skimming.

My thoughts upon you reside
Perhaps in me, you could confide
What on earth you see in me?
For I no longer am in my prime.

No matter-refreshingly lovely
Gorgeous and sexy with love to spare
Awoke my passion- this I will share
Then- against you, others cannot compare.

English Rose

Then smile for me my English rose,
Through this smile I'll write the prose,
Give joy to warm your beating heart
Find the peace you seek, from wide and far.

Then from this joy you'll blossom well
The fragrance of spring you do expel.
How calm the waters in the stomach lie
Reach out your arms, give faith one more try.

In jubilation one thirsts for the early morning dew
A pulsating beat inside, over-due or on cue?
Forgive the mind as sometimes it does flit
Hold fast the moment, let not this, through fingers slip.

Now see clear how rainbow colours shine,
How swift the birds in flight steeply climb,
How crystal clear brooks waters flow,
How one chance meeting makes you glow?

Radiating beauty from the inner soul
Feelings and emotions you cannot control,
The flush of the cheeks when one does inspire.
Perhaps by chance, is found, your desire?

Now let spring last for evermore
The harboured love is released for sure.
New courage found and thoughts no longer weak
A warm embrace, a welcome kiss upon the cheek.

Oh! English rose you have blossomed well
You have found your happiness I can tell.
The smile now is so full of strength,
With shadows dispersed, sunshine is now all that's left.

The Symphony

A melody plays in the mind
Surrounding your name like a shrine
Whispered notes float upon high
Greeted by a smile that lights up the sky.

A dream escapes from a tortured mind
Of a wish, to give sight to the blind,
Love stood just an arm's length away
And the heart beat faster, hoping you'd stay.

The chrysalis opens, the butterfly is born
Its elegant, fragile beauty forever to be won.
Captures the eyes of one who is smitten
Follows its flight, understands what fate has written.

A wind is the chorus that teases the trees
The thunder is cymbals, clashing with ease
And rainbows follow showers is what nature brings,
While love is the symphony playing the strings.

The Challenge

Supple and lithe swings in the breeze
Elegant and defined ,crisp and clean.
A beauty unsurpassed a beauty to tease
How adorable how triumphant how serene,
How sad then a beauty such as thee
Stands in the shadow of my love , my Queen.
Oh nature you bestow upon us your very best
Yet my love, in my eyes, there is no contest.
How she lights up my life with her amber glow
The love that I hold, on her I bestow.
The ache in my heart will remain until at last we meet
As with the circle of life, then I will be complete.
It only remains that she should feel the same
Her love for you the Orchid ,the challenge will remain.

You Came Alive

Silhouetted by the evening sun
Shadows cast across my eyes
Fair hair falling across your eyes,
A vision of loveliness swept across the floor.

A beaming smile and eyes that shone
Your body- sensuously provocative
Accentuating your sexiness just for me.
A warm handshake spoke more than words
Your hormones awoke as did mine.
I thought I'd like to know you, take my time.

We gelled, it was easy to tell
We wanted each other, for me that was swell.
Each time we got close, electricity flowed
You came alive and your body glowed.

Standing behind, you looked real good
I wanted to stroke you- if only I could.
Your legs are so shapely, so divine
Soon I will caress them -as you do recline.

Foolish Thoughts

A warm tender soft loving face
Eyes that leave warmth to trace
The smile that offers gentleness
And lips to promise tenderness.

Lyrical injustice for words to rhyme
Whilst your poetry in motion all of the time
Words ebb and flow as do the great sea
One day will I your harbour be?

So many times I've touched your face
On celluloid, where I can, your contours trace.
I stare deep into your lovely eyes
Try to read if there is a hidden guise.

Your lips to me an oasis be
To quench a thirst so wonderfully
To hold your face in my hands
To plant a kiss, where I have planned.

Foolish thoughts inside my head
Words that will never be said
Fear of rejection that I dread
And empty dreams and deeds lie dead.

Harmony

I'll walk through life a little while with you
Together we'll see what we both can do
Find a level that suits us both
Stay as friends or become betrothed.

We won't change our ideals in life
Take strides together don't accept any strife
Have a harmony unsurpassed
Find a comfort that we hope will last.

Too long the age we lived had wasted time
Our chance now, to share something most sublime,
Let shackles and fetters fall away
Allow freedom of emotions begin from today.

As nature calls to wayward souls
Where words and thoughts have no control
Unification, a pairing as we join the throng
Perhaps as nature intends, we belong.

When sweet darling buds?

Soft tender alabaster skin
Moon eyes that make you grin
Lips of deep cherry red fruit
Pink tongue shines like a new shoot.

Written words dispel the chill
Natures love the heart does spill
Warms the soul beneath the skin
To seek the danger is a sin.

Open arms offer warm embrace
The inviting smile requests the haste
Beguiled by youth and tender flesh
When sweet darling buds bloom the best.

Longing

Your smile delights my weary eyes
Your lips a promise- I surmise,
Your face I now know so well
My hands to touch, caress, as pleasures swell.

Your ears so soft I long to kiss
Your throat, my lips fail to miss
Your skin so soft, glows as marble sheen.
Your loveliness apparent, my joy supreme.

And what shall follow my humble words?
Supreme gestures that looks obscene?
In truth my wisdom cannot prevail
Like shadows in sunlight, I shrivel and fail.

If once we danced to the Blue Danube?
Could see reflections as the mirrors do?
If just once a lovers embrace we held
Share delight as our bodies, together weld.

A Request

May I dance with you in the moonlight?
Hold you in my arms safe and tight
Feel your warmth pressing against my chest.
Smell your perfume, as on my shoulder, your head does rest.

The music is sensuous and intoxicating
Our bodies blend together in exaltation
Freedom of bodies and minds fly high
To the astral heavens that light the sky.

Empty Awareness

Oh! Lovely lady with skin soft and warm
How come you turn to me?
With my greying hair, not as it used to be
What do you see in this old man worn?

Time has passed but I rode it true
I lost in love-that time I do rue
Alone, I withdrew from society
Kept myself true to the sobriety.

Years did pass-I stayed alone
Not entreating love- but my eyes did roam
Passion slept through each season
Soon I forgot- for no other reason.

I gazed upon many pretty women
Dormant did my heart abide
Until the time on you-my eyes spied
A fluttering thrill sent my heart skimming.

My thoughts upon you reside
Perhaps in me, you could confide
What on earth you see in me?
For I no longer am in my prime.

No matter-refreshingly lovely
Gorgeous and sexy with love to spare
Awoke my passion- this I will share
Then- against you, others cannot compare.

Mirrored Heart

Look upon this broken heart,
If you are loved then pities do
Let eyes that see true depth of love
Embrace with joyousness and wonder,
Give and receive a blessing true
Eclipse the moon and feel the sun
Mellow slowly that rancour fails to show
Feel not sadness watch as happiness grows.
Plant a thought so carefully
See as it grows so steadfastly
In strength and faith,
Through dark and light
Embrace in thought as you seek inside
The mirrored heart where you abide

Of You

A meadow full of yellowed corn
Under the cobalt blue washed sky,
A babbling brook, its waters crystal clear
Winter is in slumber and summer is here.

Fresh as the daisy, elegant as a butterfly
Warm as the summer breeze,
Blessed with the sting of a bumble bee
Yet has the strength of the spider's web.

Solid as the forge anvil
So soft as the cotton wool,
Fragile as the bone china cup
While so sensitive when tears do spill

When seasons meet and blend together
As tormented by inclement weather
Each obstacle sent to test and override
To you I turn to, in you I do confide.

Through the eyes

Oh my love- your beautiful face
A thousand words I do write
Each of love, each a delight.
To capture each flair of your skin
One has to start from deep within.

Your soul the core of life
Bubbles and boils without strife.
Yet love arrives-the heat does rise
You see through the cloudy disguise.

Once breath is torn from deep within
When tingles set about the skin.
As the mind flits and flirts
A common thought that love can hurt.

Bless our creator for this one chance,
Join together for our loves dance.
You know within that destiny has arrived
You see all this through your own eyes.

If

To close the eyes and clearly see your face,
To slumber peacefully knowing you are the grace.
When dreams contain the spiritual you
And upon awaking, find in a vision, a face so true,
With eyes that look deep into my soul
That stirs and warms the body through.
When ears long to hear some soft words
To equal treasures which have been unearthed?
The jewels from deep within earths crust
As men labour long through sweat and toil,
When angers dispelled and not despoiled.
Whilst searching out the steps you trod
With hunger for your arms to me enfold,
Yet lonely with time, slowly grow old.
But, like the jewel, never dim or age in time,
Where prisms of light twinkle bright as a star
And sweet pressed lips tells the story so far,
Would the story end, or begin, if you were mine?

Whispers

How silently the clouds drift by
How still the wind to hear the angels sigh
How sure and true is cupid's arrow
When thoughts of love had dimmed grown sallow.

Angel's attire worn gossamer thin
Carries lonely souls within
To choose a companion the task to keep
The fruits of love the harvest to reap.

Over mountains high and seas so deep
One whispered word a promised leap
The smile so wide and eyes that weep
Joy in the heart, long, a secret keep.

Each searching whisper comes from within
A joyful union now can begin
The loving hand has been offered up
Untainted love can now be supped.

How sweet your whispers float into my ear
And heartbeats sound loud and clear.
When blood does surge like molten gold
The font of love will forever unfold.

Thoughts that swirl within the head
Remembering all the words once said
This flush of joy makes light ones feet
In loving arms rest, and safely sleep.

Image of Aphrodite

Swift as the bird in full flight
Transparent as a moonbeam at night
Sweet as nectar from the bees honeycomb
Hoping that the wish comes true very soon.

Black as a raven her hair is the delight
Shines like a beacon with richness so bright,
Eyes that go deep and draws you inside
Gentleness of creatures like a fawn she does glide.

Image of Aphrodite this goddess of love
Teases and temps with the freedom of a dove,
This beauty of nature as well as the sea
Drives one to distraction with hope eternally.

The touch of her breath the smell of her perfume
Giddiness is apparent as intoxication comes too soon
Her svelte like figure passes before the eyes
Love is forever for there is no disguise.

Imagining You

Gentle rolling, lush green hills,
Warm breathe of a summer breeze
The backdrop of a cobalt blue sky.
Looking up at the heavens, emit a contented sigh.
Long, lazy days of summer,
A casual stroll through pine carpeted forests,
Peace and quiet broken by the chirping of the birds
A crack of a dried twig echoes long and loud.
Sunlight streams through the silent sentinels
Guardian of forest creatures large and small.
Did you see the pixie dance over the carpet green?
Hear the piped music yet the orchestra remained unseen.
Insects buzzing overhead flitting through the trees,
While caterpillars lounge sleepily on a juicy leaf.
Harken to the croak of a bullfrog deep inside the vale,
Smell the richness of the carpeted floor
Knowing that nobody has been there before.
Rest against the bark of an age- old tree
Stop and think what sights that might have been.
Open slowly eyes that rested through the balmy day
Remember how I see you, how I'd imagined you this way.

Sadly

Where does my heart lie now?
Betwixt heaven and Earth
Sitting upon a soft white cloud
Being caressed by the sun.
Or is it the brightness of your
Welcoming smile? Or
Eyes that shine in merriment,
And twinkle as the stars.
The depth of which escapes me
Which is of no surprise,
I know that I am welcome
For you do not disguise
Or pretend you have
No interest, I do think
In that you are so wise.
You offer a smile to greet me
And you speak softly yet
Seductively for the huskiness
You just cannot hide.
All the while my senses are reeling
I've lost control of my feelings.
Then sadly I wake up
And know I've only been dreaming.

Missing the Music

There is no zing
No silent pang
No heartbeats fast, forever to last,
No pulse to race, or last the pace.
Shiny eyes that brim with hope,
Instead the silence where thoughts evoke
A memory that brings a tear
And emptiness became a thing to fear.
When light did shine
And had warmth from the sun,
As music gave life to each and everyone
When two solo artists became as one
Then orchestras joined in as the whole world spun,
Where feet did dance to the selected tune
And the people there began to bloom,
As flowers open to the strings delight
Whilst babbling brooks shared in their delight
When nature fawned and began to swoon
And life was good until night came in far too soon.
Now damp and chilled, warmth has all been spilled
Hollowed eyed and sallow skin
Drained of joy as sadness creeps slowly in
Heavy legged and heavy heart
Missing the music, the true tempo of life
Darkened skies and chilled winds brings strife
The orchestra fades, and sadly the solo artist's part.

Plain Walls

No pictures adorn my inner walls
As from grace in family eyes I did fall
Cast aside my use its course did run
The raw emotion now leaves me numb.

Who knows what idea was conceived
To bring about such selfish greed,
Pretence flowed like a mountain stream
Playing happy families, her success indeed.

Broken hearts her evil took
But inside she bubbled as a brook
Taking all was her actual gain
Regardless of the children's pain.

Now broke and empty outside I stand
The love and trust now lifeless, bland.
Time has cast its shadow well
Heartache is a heavy load to you I tell.

Silence closes in as a trap
Inside my head their voices still do chat,
Yet no pictures are hung upon my walls
As longing for their love, teardrops fall.

In You

What beauty do I see in you?
A smile, and eyes bright and true,
A welcome look from deep within
In search for love, chapter of life to begin?

A complexion marble smooth yet so soft
Whose lips entice so full and prim.
This face so warm offers a welcome too.
What pleasures await a coyness in sin?

I lay beside your picture sweet
My dreams relaxed a comfort keep.
Inside your head I rest and sleep
Yet I disturb- intrude- as my presence is felt.

Elastic Minds

Have I missed you, I know not why
Did we have a rendezvous, if so why?
Memory is so fickle
It flits from here to there,
For what the eyes do see- the mind simply doesn't care.

Your face is so familiar
It strikes a cord or two
And the caring smile,
Oh, I just wonder, is it really you?

I do recall your soft touch
And a whisper in my ear,
Then the mist surrounds me
But dear oh dear- if I only knew?

The rain rattles on the roof
And the windows are all streaky
Yet, as I walk across the floor
The sound I hear is all squeaky.

The days are getting longer,
Nights getting shorter still
As soon as I am asleep
I'm woken to take another pill.

I have to go now my dear
I'll see you to the door,
The answer to your question?
How long you'll stay in here, I really am not sure.

Two Trysts

The first love, truly everlasting love
Each painful step that took them apart
Forever anchored within their hearts
Never forgotten, seeking out the special one.

Where deep inside the hidden pain
Recaptures the ending again and again
Memory holds the face once so dear
Shows the heartache crystal clear.

Recalled in that moment of pain
When tears stung like acid rain
As distance between them greater became.
End of the tryst, both carried the shame.

Yet years have passed and memories linger,
The joy and pain no less dimmer
Oh face return, let eyes, the smile remember,
One hopes for the spark again to glimmer.

Forever Entwined

Lay my love, lay with me
Embrace the warmth that comforts thee.
Rest your head on pillows of down
Soothe from worry, your troubled brow.

Sleep my love a dreamless sleep
Troubles away from you I'll keep.
Refresh both body and mind
No torment here will you find.

A gentle sleep to ease your woes
I will guard against all foes
For in your tranquil slumber
In my mind I will wonder.

You, here with me
How I wonder this to be
Yet staid and firm I will stand
Forever to give a helping hand.

My love and strength I shall give
As long as we both shall live.
And as age slowly takes its grip
Hands entwined they will not slip.

Misty Mornings

Father oh Father
How eerie the silence sounds
How cold and damp when misty mornings dawn
Encased in wood now for eternity
Yet my eyes still see as mortal once was I.

Lost, I roam through swirls of gossamer strands
Where shadows lurk to steal my sight
Yet still I seek that which I was denied
An anchor to cradle my beating heart.

As once with love I stood so tall
An oak to be leaned upon
Then cast aside as flotsam upon the mighty sea
Seeking haven and pride, salvation
Searching out an identity, seeking me.

Blown like a leaf in tumultuous winds
I met my doom
Empty hands reached out to those I'd loved
Now in your bosom do I lay.

My flesh will rot, bones crumble to dust
Cold damp sod envelopes my case of wood
And as each misty morning eclipses the night
My soul cries in pain for just one more sight
Those that I gave life, one smile a wish that gives a father delight.

Empty Memories

O come my children
Seek out he who created you,
He who suffers at your hands
Turns the other cheek at rumours
That burns deep into his soul.
How turmoil ebbs and flows
Inside a head that seeks only peace.
Who turned your love into hate?
Forbade the tongue of truth
And seared your heart?
What memories do you still hold?
Happy times have now gone so cold,
Those smiles once free and so full of cheer
Gone forever just like your love.
Yet still he holds you both so near
Even though each night he sheds a tear.
Of what is missed those smiles so sweet.
Kisses that swept him off his feet.
And hands that trusted him so dear
When together there was no fear.
Like the photo now dimmed with time
Staring blankly where youth will never age
Now grown in years your features fade
Whilst recognition dims with age.
Futures hazy and he cannot cope,
But still an empty heart cries in hope.

Turned Emotions

As lyrics and music compliment each other
So man and woman should be together.
Love and hate, good and bad
Hope and joy happy, glad
You and me apart we're both sad
Pain and sorrow, is there a tomorrow?
Empty, full aches and pains, deep sorrow.
Where laughter and smiles, coo as the dove
Turned to a different emotion, grew to love
Those aches and pains remain
Images carried in the mind
Shown through the naked eye
Yet still the pain stays
Where once a smile would make a day
When night- time comes it has gone away.
Now eat, just eat for comforts sake
Appetite lost, the hunger for something food cannot sate.
Love is blind, yet clear I see
I've found a love for eternity.

Effecting a mind

Oh! Sadness becomes me.
She walks out the door and dreams are shattered
The smile I like remains with me
But she has gone, out of my life?

Oh! Sadness becomes me.
How calm the voice, how soft the eyes
How affected have I become?
Implanted now in my mind
One who I feel is so kind.

Foolish to believe she likes me, but is hope?
Thoughts are mine to contemplate
Dreams are for the lonely
As in limbo and darkness with no scope.

Calm and assured I will remain
Not letting on she is to blame.
For the chaos-turbulence she has caused
As slowly she turns, for me she has paused.?

Eyes meet-her pupils dilate
Have I missed the opportunity?
Did she purposely hesitate?
I stumble and stall-fail to have impunity.

I declare-I swear- if granted
Offer the open heart despoiled,
Broken but waiting to be recoiled
Feel warmth and tender feelings replanted.

Fair maiden sweet
I declare and entreat,
Grant one boon- your company
One day-one night my pleasure be.

I adore your smile-I'm lost within your eyes
Your voice is soft-mellow and entrancing.
Your hair so soft and shining,
Your hands elegant and tender
Lost within your being my heart I must render.

Oh! Sadness becomes me,
My inner thoughts I have surrendered,
My consciousness lies bare and open,
My tortured heart needs caressing.

My eyes need to drink in your beauty
My hands need to clasp your hands
My arms need to embrace you
My lips need to kiss those of yours.

Yet ghost like images wrap around me
Their tendrils confuse my eyes
I reach for you- you are not there,
I hear your voice-diminishing in the mist.
Alone I stand-without the memory of a kiss.

Offering

This beauty I see
Hangs from a thread
Within the minds eye,
Of shallow pretences
Or of gossamer absence?
Merely a trick
From a magicians wand
A thought to give credence
A smile to make sense.
No importance am I
In Gods given eye.
But before me you stand
Offering your hand
Then how can it be
That I cannot flee
Burdened by chains
So shall I remain?
Awaiting the date
Of destination my fate.

Flawed Hope

Mere mortal am I
Not like a mystical God
Now long forgotten
A rough uncut diamond
Unpolished and coarse
Flawed for a time
Then I met you
With steel and water
Shaped and polished I became
But alas, a dark vein did run
Through the centre
That saddened
And spoilt your work
Away you turned
Unfinished, incomplete
I stood alone
The sparkle gone
The fire doused
Grey ashes left
That scattered in the wind.

When words fail

How feelings do ebb and flow,
Seeing your eyes brightly aglow
With passion held deep within
You show the world you have no sin.
When stood tall and head held high
Eyes that search the clear blue sky
Your hopes and dreams your endless search,
Your trials and triumphs others try to besmirch.
While your heart seeks the haven to savour
To mirror deeds, thoughts and behaviour.
One that brings the gleam to your lovely eyes
Who offers all with truth, no shadows or disguise.
As body gestures seem to tell the tale,
When everything is right, yet words do fail
Then cherish he who offers this
The price required, is that of one sweet kiss.

Should I?

Should I leave you when pain is rife?
When darkness in my heart does bite,
And icy fingers clasp my soul
And a waterfall of tears I cannot control.

Should I wait to see again your smiling face?
Or lose myself in a crowded place,
In knowing you, true love I knew
Like a flower it blossomed and it grew.

Should I stay and fight for you?
With words deeds and honour too
Whilst in another's arms you do slumber
The grief I feel tears my soul asunder.

Should I cease from loving you?
For this pain and hurt is all so true.
Too late I found I fell in love
Too late a dream was not enough.

Dreadful Fear

In the deepest recesses of the mind
Where the fear of loneliness lurks,
Behind the memories wrapped in sheer delight,
Where, as the twilight years inexorably beckon
And the parting of ways leaves one mortally stricken.

How does one fight this dreadfully awful dilemma?
If no-one listens or bothers to care.
Should a life be turned to dust forever?
For it was unrequited love, one not shared.

The simple greed of green it seemed
Stole the heart along with the dream.
Left empty shells, discarded upon the darkened path,
Where shadows formed, the depths which forever would last.

Fearful Companion

It passed through like a shadow in the night
Silent and transparent yet it caught the eyesight
A chill ran down the once warm spine
And the dry forehead soon began to shine.

Hands would soon begin to lose their grip
Legs would tremble and feet start to slip.
Breathing is hoarse and comes in gasps
Heartbeat rises knowing they cannot last.

Fear is a companion fright is another name.
Yet who instilled this teaching?
It is they who hold the blame
While in the head someone is still preaching.

The subject has no substance,
No solid form to grasp or feel.
Yet unknown terror grips with just a glance.
Can the mind oppose something that isn't real?

From Whence we came

I started from a speck of dust
And grew into the man you once knew
We shared both in love and trust
Which grew stronger with each passing year?
Until one day a cowardly act turned love into fear.
As cancer grows inside a shell
So hatred spawns and greed does swell.
The cynical plans to destroy your life
Considered deliberately and precise
Conjured up by both mother and wife
Left us broken hearted ,and full of strife.
No father now to turn for aid
No daughters now to prepare for life.
Held fast in shadows where no smiles are played
As blinded by the lies she has sprayed
For riches gained portray her true desire
Whilst offspring's flesh and blood slowly expire.
Through trauma's rent the broken heart
And slowly as the image fades through time apart
Standing by a grave stone, he died of a broken heart
The words "Did he know we loved him"
Echo's against the swirling mist
For he knew no love from those he missed
Returned to dust a spectre he
Seeks out their love and forgiveness, through eternity.

An ill wind blows

When the heart feels the gentle tug,
As eyes ponder as to where to look
And hands talk at speeds that cannot prevail,
Whilst minds whisper yet words do fail.
Then hope disappears when the door is closed.

Just a slip in time to cast the spell
Through times past one wonders ,well
What is there to keep one sane?
A heart beats faster is it all in vain?
Thoughts remain to hold one tight
To surrender easily without a fight.

Yet deep within the answer lies
From trembling palms to hope that flies
Infatuation seems the answer here
Though these feelings inside, are so sincere
Those eyes that draw one in so deep
While her lovely smile remains until one sleeps.

 So who is there to tell the truth?
Of how the feelings bare but so uncouth,
With awe and wonder in brief moments filled
Whose once warm heart is then somewhat chilled
 An ill wind blows just as fate decrees,
Ones hopes are dashed ,like wind blown leaves.

And standing bleak amidst four stone walls,
Echo's the sound of sadness as failure calls
Bowed and broken but with spirit full of hope
To win the ladies heart with vision and a wider scope.

Encouraged by the beating heart, seeing eyes that burn so bright
Those that guide me to my hearts delight.
Until the dreadful words are passed from those sweet lips.
And the fire that burns dies to ashes, leaving dreams eclipsed.

A Last Goodbye

And words are so useless unless spoken from the heart,
When eyes look deep and a smile leaves the lips apart.
As a body aches and whilst the soul does cry,
Still the mind does throb, and from the throat a sigh.

Tormented and teased to the extreme, whilst unappeased
An emotional face shown leaving none too displeased.
Now stung by acrid tears leave marked furrows on dry cheeks.
Rejection is haunting, daunting, price of love is never cheap.

Through glazed eyes one sees them turn and slowly disappear.
The drawn out words of a last goodbye still lingers in the ear.
A gentle breeze blows through for they are no longer there,
The pain feels constant- and again the heart lies bare.

The Final Kiss

Is this then, the final kiss?
The one that says the sad goodbye
To mingle with a salty tear
The one that brings to life our greatest fear
Eyelashes heavy with globes of teardrops
Misty visions distorted by confusion
Heartbeats race and palms get sweaty
Whilst the mouth goes dry and it's hard to swallow?

The sun has sunk and now deep shadows form
Disorientated due to emotional turmoil
Like a cloak the heartache in silence is heavily worn
What happened to those words once sacredly sworn?
Those guilty secrets that lay behind the false smile.
Where once a paragon, through which the bright light did shine
Now dimmed forever, tainted and defiled.
Should words ease the tempest deep within
Use hollow actions to pardon the sin?

Ingram Content Group UK Ltd.
Milton Keynes UK
UKHW012009140323
418553UK00004B/306